MY CEMETERY FRIENDS

MY CEMETERY FRIENDS

A GARDEN OF ENCOUNTERS AT MOUNT SAINT MARY IN QUEENS, NEW YORK

BY

VINCENT J. TOMEO

atmosphere press

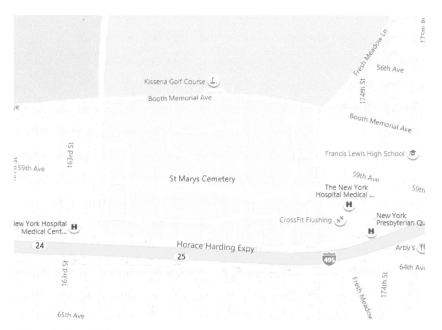

Figure 1: Google Map

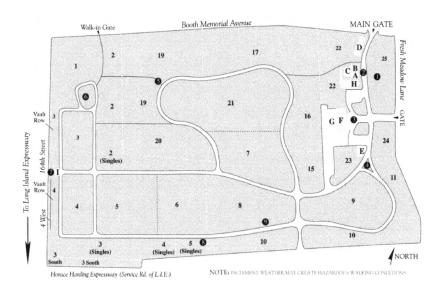

Figure 2: Mt. St. Mary Cemetery

172-00 Booth Memorial Avenue, Flushing, New York 11365

TABLE OF CONTENTS

DEDICATION

This book is dedicated to the ten soldiers from Corona, Queens who were killed in the Vietnam War, and also pays homage to all those who gave their last full measure of devotion in defense of our freedom. I honor their extraordinary gallantry. May they Rest in Peace and everlasting dignity.

Corona's Stone Memorial of Ten Heroes: Ten Heroes Plaza, Triangle Park in Corona, 108th Street between Van Doren Street and Westside Avenue, Corona, NY 11368

Specialist, Fourth-Class, U.S. Army
Anthony Victor Campaniello
10/11/1946 – 12/19/1967

Pvt. First-Class, U.S. Army
Charles Philip De Tomaso
11/27/1946 – 04/29/1967

Specialist, Fourth-Class, U.S. Army
Randolph A. Edwards

08/27/1946 – 02/07/1968
Lance Corporal, U.S. Marine Corps
Charles William Eglin, III
06/02/1947 – 02/15/1968

Pvt. First-Class, U.S. Army
Leandro Garcia
08/02/1946 – 02/02.1968

Pvt. First-Class, U.S. Army
William Earl Gray
10/14/1947 – 02/16/1967

Pvt. First-Class, U.S. Army
Vernell Owens
01/02/1945 – 04/17/1968

Pvt. First-Class, U.S. Army
Charles Victor Piccolella
02/14/1944 – -/-/1966

Corporal, U.S. Army
Benjamin Robert Turian
11/10/1945 – 03/24/1969

Sergeant, U.S. Army
Robert Joseph Zerille
09/03/1947 – 09/11/1968

INTRODUCTION

I am interested in both the living and the dead because they remind me of how to live.

This book honors all the deceased who are interred in Mount Saint Mary Cemetery, as well as all those who gave their last full measure of devotion in honor and service to our nation, the United States of America, and are buried here and elsewhere. We honor them, and we pay homage to them. My story is a documentation, an eye-witness account of my walks through the cemetery for more than thirty-three years.

My Cemetery Friends is a compilation of new beginnings, of friendships and acquaintances made, of history, and of knowledge gained, as I trekked through the cemetery, which, to me, is a garden. I think a cemetery is also a place where one can experience six degrees of separation, by meeting people through other people. It is interesting how one connection, even in a graveyard, can have far-reaching effects. *My Cemetery Friends* celebrates life and comes full circle, starting with my encounter with Father Romano A. Zanon standing on a grave in the rain, and ends with his burial, his entombment in a cremation niche in a mausoleum and my continuing journey. Walk with me through the cemetery, see this garden, and share the encounters, joys, and histories.

MY CEMETERY FRIENDS

I found a pen on a grave in Mount Saint Mary Cemetery just when I needed one and went to my car to retrieve some paper. I had to decide where I would compose *My Cemetery Friends*. The closest place to my heart in this cemetery was my mother's grave, so I sat in the shade there. It was a warm Saturday afternoon in May, and the colors of the flowers brought to mind a poem I titled "How Many Colors in a Day?"

How Many Colors in A Day?

Dawn,
Moon-blue, scarlet, lemon-yellow.

Morning,
Silver, gold, cornflower-blue.

Mid-day,
Jungle-green, primrose-yellow, sky-blue.

Afternoon,
Burnt umber, white, gold, marine blue.

Evening,
Light-gray, flaming-white, cobalt-blue.

Midnight,
Moon lily-white, ebony-black, darkest blue.

A full day—variegated.

A cemetery can be an inspirational environment in which to write a poem. The birds were singing. A cool breeze was so refreshing since I live in an overcrowded, noisy section of Flushing, Queens. I sat under a tree near my mother's grave and started to write. While writing, I noticed a man, three rows away. He was dressed all in black and walked to a grave where he got down on his knees, transfixed like a statue for maybe fifteen minutes. I looked up and saw him lying on the grave. The man's head and shoulders were just off the ground. Such theatrics were startling to me.

Four rows away, a woman was standing for a very long time. At her feet were seedlings, a shovel, and a spade; she held a watering can in her hand. She was looking up, perhaps taking in the sun. She seemed to be in a trance.

Five rows away from her was another woman digging up dirt on a grave. A young man stood beside her. Perhaps her son. Off in the distance, I heard bagpipes playing. It was not the first time I'd heard bagpipes there. Many times, when I happen to the cemetery, I listen to the same bagpipe music played by the same bagpiper but different melodies at different times. I come to the cemetery often. I find it a peaceful place to exercise in an otherwise chaotic, cacophonous urban environment. Here, there are no cars, very few people, no crowds, no noise, fresh air, birds singing, and colorful flowers. The grass is clean, healthy, and cut. Flowers are popping up their little heads, everywhere. Yes, the cemetery is a garden.

It is so quiet and peaceful here. I sat under a tree and started writing, wondering where that music was coming from as it floated through the air like clouds—faint, lovely, triumphant music. The music was sweet to hear. Who was playing the bagpipes? Where and why? My curiosity was piqued. I started to follow the sound and let my ears lead the way to where the music was emanating from. The music filled the cemetery with patriotic, peaceful, and joyous melodies. This time, I was going to find out who was playing it, where, and why. Off I went walking amid the tombstones to face the music. Meandering through the patterned cemetery plots and headstones, I saw a man standing on a grave playing heart-touching music, but I did not want to disturb him. I paused to listen, and this filled me with a sad, sweet feeling of a holy sort. I did not want to interrupt him. I walked away. On another day, I heard him play again. I listened to the birds chirping as the breeze whipped up and the clouds rolled in. He stood still, like a statue on a grave. This time, he was standing on a different plot in a separate section of the cemetery. Why, I wondered? I had to find out.

Gingerly I walked up to him and waited for him to finish playing. I asked him why he was playing the bagpipes on different graves. He told me it was his way of honoring those who gave their lives for America, and he went from tomb to grave. Veterans, firefighters, police officers. He is paying his respect. Paying tribute to the fallen unsung heroes that few people know, or recognize, and how could they, on an individual basis, as there are just too many. Here, this man was taking it upon himself to acknowledge each person, honoring them with a bagpipe tribute, almost every other day.

I thought to myself, this was a gracious and noble act of human kindness. As a poet, I thought his way of honoring the dead was commendable. Just think. He pays homage and remembers people he does not know, and this is stunning. It is sheer poetry!

Music Ambles Drunk with Sorrow

A lone man stands, dressed in a Scotch kilt,
playing bagpipes, pouring whiskey over a grave.
A moon casts shadows of dancing clouds,
music ambles drunk with sorrow.

He stands desolate, like a tree on a vengeful African
    Savanna,
prominent, eerie, petrified, alone.
His footprints leave a mark standing on freshly laid sod.
A playful wind defiantly blows his auburn-red hair.

A forgiving Sun crowns his head,
as light washes his face against a cobalt-blue sky.
This chalk-white man is turning blood red,
as his cheeks rise blowing on his bagpipes.
Quickly his fingers move as if he were playing a piano
    concerto.
The music is triumphant, not belligerent,
fills pensive air like a motet.
Sweet, holy music hovers over a city of the dead.

Now he is trembling in grief,
as glorious music reached a dominant piercing pitch.

A Hallelujah moment!

A lone man stands, dressed in a Scotch kilt,
playing bagpipes, pouring whiskey over a grave.
A moon casts shadows of dancing clouds,
music ambles drunk with sorrow.

I wanted to learn more about him. I learned that his name is Mr. Joe Baker. He was a former firefighter and lives on Jewel Avenue in Flushing, a section of Queens. Like me, Mr. Baker finds the cemetery to be a sanctuary, a rustic retreat, and a peaceful place to ponder. Often when I do my daily walking, I hear him play. I don't want to disturb him, but if he sees me, he will stop to acknowledge me. "Hello, Red!" Since he is not good at remembering names, he calls me by the color of my hair. It is also my nickname: "Red."

On other occasions, Mr. Joe Baker spoke to me about many things: current events, poetry, 9/11, and history. Love to listen to him play his bagpipes. For now, I must keep on moving, as I came here to exercise and not to chitchat. Have to keep on circling the cemetery trail and pick up my pace.

MEANDERING THROUGH THE CEMETERY

It was a foggy and misty day in 1988 just two days after the death of my beloved mother, Antoinette Eloise Tomeo. My mother was such a kind, caring, and strong lady. I could write a book about her struggles. Through it all, Mama persevered. I was filled with sweet sorrow, and joy, just thinking of Mama.

Over the Fence

Mama!
Every day for five years,
I visited your grave.

One Christmas day,
I was late.

The cemetery gates were locked.
Climbed a bronze fence,
left my tracks in the snow.

Mama, I miss your smiling face, laughter, and songs. I will always carry you in my heart forever. Mama, I wrote this poem for you:

Mama's Slippers

Mama's fuzzy slippers were sinking,
Like Salvador Dalí's painting, "The Persistence of
    Memory,"
Her time is wrapped, hung down, bent over, exhausted.
Seems to hug, clasp, embrace the back of her favorite
    chair.

Mama's fuzzy slippers are light, smoothly worn,
spongy, soft, squeezable.
Shaped like a small Indian boat,
Yellow, brown interwoven wool.

A playful wool ball crowned the instep of Mama's
    slippers.

Mama's slippers could fit the feet of a ballerina
in an interlude from an opera.

Out of the blue, Mama would say,
"When I die, make sure my feet are warm,"
I would pretend not to listen.

Mama died, realized listened.

I gave the funeral director Mama's slippers.
I thought no more of it.
Mama buried.
Slippers returned.

Whenever I hold Mama's slippers,
my heart is filled with warm, sweet joy.

I remember the smell of her perfume.

The clouds were gathering, forming like the Grand Army of the Republic, blue and gray. Heavy clouds were marching in. As fog hung overhead like a pall, I was inspired to write this poem:

Fog

It oozed in during the night,
blurred light blocked sight.
The day became night.

Jungle's morning moisture mix.
Teardrops dew,
marked day in doubt.

We wondered what to do.

I noticed a priest standing over a grave, one lone priest, a casket, and no one else. This touched me. It started to drizzle. Nevertheless, I walked over to the cemetery plot and lowered my head to say a prayer. I remained there for the whole service. Afterward, the priest asked, "Are you family? Did you know her?" "No," I said, "I just felt someone should honor this person. There is no one here." I didn't know then that my friendship with this priest would last for over three decades.

He asked me whether I came here often. I said, "Yes, mostly to exercise and to stop at my mother's grave." He again asked me what compelled me to stop and pray in the rain on a foggy day for a stranger. I told him it is up to us, the living, to honor the dead. He asked me if he could come to my mother's grave and bless her. I think this was his way of saying thank you.

As we walked to my mother's grave on the other side of the cemetery, we talked. He asked, "What is your profession?" I told him, "See that school in the distance? I teach there." He said he knew Francis Lewis High School and was counseling several troubled students who attended my school. At the grave, the Reverend Father Romano A. Zanon performed a blessing and recited a few prayers. After that, we parted, and I continued my walk. I didn't know where the Father went, and I thought this would be the last time we would speak or meet. I was wrong. Often walking through the cemetery, I saw the Reverend Father Romano A. Zanon giving the Last Rites and performing services at gravesites. After funeral services, I would stop, say hello, and sometimes we would have a long conversation.

Over two or three years, I found out much more about this priest and who he was. One day I asked him, "Father, what made you become a priest?" He told me he was in the Korean War in the Battle of the Chosin Reservoir and almost froze to death. Father Romano A. Zanon told me he prayed to God that if he and the other soldiers survived, he would devote his life to God. He told me he prayed for all those who lost their lives in the Korean War. I asked him what he did in the Army. He said he was a combat infantry soldier and a photographer who documented the horrors of the Korean War. He told me to come to the chapel office the following Friday, and he would share with me photographs that recorded his time in Korea.

Friday came, and I waited outside the chapel door until after the services were over. Then, Father Romano A. Zanon invited me into the chapel office and unlocked a desk drawer. He took out a massive photo album. Inside that album, history came alive. Father Zanon had documented the Korean War. I told Father Zanon I was a history teacher and had a great interest in the Korean War. We spent over three hours peering over fantastic, museum-quality photos of the Korean War, of Korean refugees, tens of thousands of them pouring in from the North, villages destroyed, and the capital city of South Korea, Seoul, in ruins. There were photographs of gardens, temples, lotus ponds, and several photos of Father Zanon with a lovely Korean woman, hand in hand. She was stunning, absolutely stunning. I was shocked.

He told me this was all before the Battle of the Chosin Reservoir, and she has a special place in his heart, even today. Father Zanon spoke of how he fell in love with the Korean people, and that he prays for them every day. He often wonders what happened to people in his photographs, all the people he once knew, both Koreans and the Americans with whom he served in the Armed Forces. His stories touched me. Moved by his remembrances and his photographs, my appreciation of his humanity and my respect for him grew. He was a different man from the one I assumed him to be on the day we met, but then, we never really know a person, do we?

All of us have stories. The Reverend Father Romano A. Zanon's story is worth telling. It is extraordinary, and his photographs must be shared with the world, especially with the Americans and the Koreans. I said to him I could not erase his pictures from my mind. I suggested that he donate the photos to a museum, or maybe the Korean Cultural Society in New York City, or the American–Korean War Museum. Every time he showed me the photographs, I felt I was there walking through history. He told me he was going to will the photos to his nephew in California. I said, "Father, please don't. They belong to history." He seemed to insist that his nephew should have them.

I tried to press him about the photos many times. I asked, "Does your nephew have an appreciation for history? Would he conceive of giving them a proper place in history?" The Reverend Father Romano A. Zanon said he would think about it and said no more about his nephew and what he would do with his spectacular photographs.

*

On one occasion, I told Father Zanon that I was a poet, and was having a poetry reading and slide presentation at the Bayside Public Library. My flyer of the poetry reading and slide presentation read: "Let's Celebrate Life: 'Walk with me into a poem. Sit within the space. Sail into words like whitewater rapids.'"

Father Zanon asked, "What makes a poem read well?"

I replied, "It resonates like bells long after the ringing has stopped."

At the event, while reading my poems, I noticed Father Zanon sitting attentively in the back of the auditorium. Afterward, Father and I went out for coffee. I asked him, "Father! How did you enjoy the poetry presentation?"

He said, "It was good. May I give you some suggestions? Poetry is like a photograph. You have to capture the mood. You have to move the lens to different angles. Focus and capture feelings and expressions and leave it open to interpretation. Your poetry is good, but you are holding back your emotion, and something is missing. Show your feelings. 'Poetry is feeling,' as William Blake said."

His advice stayed with me, and I learned much from his valuable criticism. Over a cup of coffee, we bonded and became friends. After that, I would walk over to the chapel and share a poem with him. Father Zanon compared poetry to photographs. He said poetry captures a moment in time with words, like photography does with pictures.

Yes, we spoke about everything from the Korean War to many other things. Father Zanon would often say, "Come to the chapel. Partake in the ceremony." But I was not interested. The Reverend Father Romano A. Zanon knew my weak spot.

One day he said, "Do you have any poetry with Christian sensibility? If you do, I would like to read them. I would like you to do a poetry reading in the chapel after the Mass." I was thrilled, but I had to sit through the Mass before the poetry reading, and that was an ordeal for which I was not ready. But a poet would do almost anything for a reading. So, I showed up, sat in the back, and after the service, Father introduced me and called me up to the podium on the altar. I read the following poems to the audience in the small chapel:

My Father's Hands

He put his hands over his eyes
He did not want to see

He put his hands out to catch me
He put his hands up in the air to let me know I was not in
    danger

He put his hands behind his back to surprise me
He put his hands on his head to play

He opened his hands to hug me
Big
My father's hands

Pieta

Robes flow like liquid cascading down a mountain
Intertwined between mother and son

In Michelangelo's brilliant eyes
He is convincingly real
Mother's profound grief masterfully composed

Trial on her face
Shocked saddened strong
Poised psychic powers
Captured in a statue's release from marble's tomb
Sculpture alive noble with a soul
Spirit's agony chiseled for eternity

She is everyone's mother
He is everyone's son
It is hard to watch a statue cry

Crucified

Dangled from a Cross
a rope made to pull the lungs into the upper throat
choking nailed to a piece of wood
flesh ripped, black iron hammered through bone,
exude marrow

Trapped, suffering, burned, bruised, bleeding,
Stomach pierced a spear plunged through his side.
Heart in his mouth
He struggles not to drown in his blood,
as raw metal seared his bare feet.

Gaze at hatred, sorrow, disgrace.

Then,
A resurrection!

The outstanding acoustics resonated my words like a bell. Afterward, they asked questions, and they wanted copies of my poems.

As the decades passed, I began to notice marked changes in Father Zanon's personality and his memory. Then, for several months, he was nowhere to be seen. I inquired in the office, and they told me that he had to retire to a sanctuary, Cathedral Seminary Residence of the Immaculate Conception Douglaston for retired priests.

When I saw him last, he did not recognize me and was somewhat hostile. I realized then that he was ill. He was not in touch with reality. He was losing his memory, or shall I say he was falling into an abyss, in and out of existence. All the decades that I had known him, I had never seen him like this. I often wonder what happens to someone who suffers from such a disease. What is it like to lose your identity, your memory of who you are, and your past? Now, when I walk through the cemetery, I sometimes think of our conversations, his insight and constructive criticism on my poetry helped me greatly. Much more, of course, I miss our friendship, his stories, his devotion to the sick, suffering, and dying. He was such an exemplary human being. I remember when I established a scholarship at Francis Lewis High School, he made a contribution. Several times he invited me into the chapel to read poetry. I remember his photographs, which left an indelible impression on my mind and heart.

He had a way of drawing out the best in people. I miss him.

Now when I pass the chapel, it's just a cold, quiet place for which I no longer have feelings. I often stop in the administrative office to inquire and ask Mr. Thomas McGrail about the Reverend Father Romano A. Zanon to find out how he is doing. I asked the director, "If and when the inevitable happens, please inform me. I want to pay my respect, read some poems I once read in the chapel, at his grave. I think he would like that." I gave the director my phone number, my email address, and copies of the poems.

I discovered much through walking the cemetery. My encounters with people have caused me to ponder over questions on life, death, and legacy, which I had never thought much about before. What an enjoyable experience to have had such a good friend. My life has been rewarded and enriched for having known him.

ANOTHER WALKING OCCASION

One sunny day in late March, the sky was clear and the air was clean. At a gravesite, I saw something twinkling in the sunlight. I stopped in my tracks and walked over to the tomb of LCPL Michael D. Glover, U.S. Marine, and there saw his Purple Heart. I could not understand why his Purple Heart was on his tombstone. I went to my car to retrieve a pad and pen, and on his grave, wrote this poem:

Reflections on a Purple Heart

On the grave of a soldier I saw
a golden medallion gleam in the light
like lightning in a storm
resting on a ledge of a gray tombstone
Bravo, 1/25 4 Marine Division,
Iraqi Freedom '06
LCPL Michael D. Glover,
The United States Marine Corps
January 19, 1978–August 16, 2006
A rock holds down his Marine patch
A Purple Heart placed on his monument bakes in the hot
    sun
and I stopped to say Thank You

After writing this poem, I lowered my head, said a prayer, and thanked Michael for so much. That night I typed up the verse and laminated it. The next time I returned to his gravesite, I placed it on the tombstone and I continued my walk through the cemetery. Two weeks later, I noticed the Purple Heart was gone.

Two months later, Memorial Day in the late afternoon, I stopped at Michael's grave with a friend who was accompanying me on my walk. We were standing at the gravesite.

Suddenly, a petite lady stepped out of her car and walked toward us. "Did you know Michael?" she asked.

I said, "No, I did not know Michael. I am the man who wrote the poem, 'Reflections on a Purple Heart,' and placed it on his grave."

She said, "Thank you," and she started crying. She told us the whole story of how he died and about his body being shipped home like a mummy.

Mrs. Margaret Glover, Michael's mother, was so appreciative and kept thanking us profusely for remembering her son. As she got into her car and drove away, I pulled out my pad and pen, and standing at Michael's gravesite, I wrote this poem:

I Visited the Grave of Marine Michael D. Glover

Memorial Day 2013 standing on Michael's grave
A petite Irish-American lady got out of her car said,

"Were you his friend?"

"Did you know him?"
No, I said,
I am the poet who wrote a poem and placed it on his grave,
Reflections on a Purple Heart.

"What a handsome boy he was," she said
"He was such a good-looking boy, well traveled, well loved,
        well educated."
She told the story how the military held his body for ten days
His face wrapped in white cloth like a mummy
How the casket had to be closed
What does one say to a mother standing on her son's grave?

Tears rolled down her face
What can one say to a mother who lost a child?
I thought I would cry
I thought my knees would cave in
I felt my heart ripping
I felt a massive lump like a rock between my heart and my
        throat
What does one say to a mother standing on her son's grave?

I lowered my head, saluted, ran my fingers across his name,
said goodbye
"Thank you," she said, "for remembering."
I saw her drive away.

How many more mothers must lose a child?
What does one say to a mother who lost a child?

That night at home, I typed the poem "I Visited the Grave of Marine Michael D. Glover," and submitted it to a poetry anthology along with "Reflections on a Purple Heart." Both poems were published. When I received the collection, I mailed them to Mrs. Margaret Glover. Mrs. Glover was so thankful that her son was made immortal in three literary anthologies. And now, the U.S. Marine Michael D. Glover has a place in literary history.

She was so appreciative that she wrote me a thank-you letter. Every Christmas, we correspond. She sends me yuletide greetings and I do the same. I hope to live to see the day when there is world peace, and a mother or father, brother or sister, spouse, or child never has to bury a loved one who has died to defend their country. I will never forget my encounter on the grave of LCPL Michael D. Glover, U.S. Marine, with his mother, Mrs. Margaret Glover. It will stay with me forever. What do you say to a mother standing at the gravesite of her son? The cemetery is a stage set for a written script. We are all actors just passing through. One never knows what kind of human contact we will make.

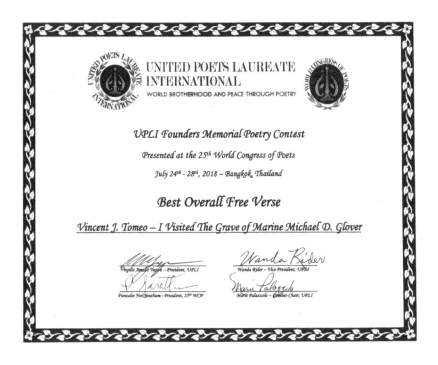

In July 2018, I won the United Poets Laureate International: World Brotherhood and Peace Through Poetry Founders Memorial Poetry Contest, the award presented at the 25th World Congress of Poets, for my poem, "I Visited the Grave of U.S. Marine Michael D. Glover." This poem is now internationally acclaimed.

With the monetary prize I was awarded, I had a brick engraved and embedded in the winding pathways of Semper Fidelis Memorial Park overlooking the National Museum of the United States Marine Corps. This brick pays homage to Michael D. Glover and the 244th birthday of the United States Marines.

THE CEMETERY IS AN OPEN BOOK

The cemetery is like an open book, filled with many stories, different people of different ethnic back- grounds, races, and occupations. I have had various encounters with different people, and I have discovered much. Walking through the cemetery, one can encounter pleasant surprises. One can establish lifelong friendships with other people. The cemetery is also a study about the immigrants in American history in encapsulated form, set in stone. Each headstone tells a story. Most of the engraved tombstones give a name, date, birth, and sometimes the event that took a life. For example:

Paul Robert Echna
April 18, 1973 – Sept. 11, 2001
Killed in the attack on the World Trade Center, Tower
#1

Or Henry Seuffert, who has a flat stone marker in obscurity under a tree. It reads:

Henry Seuffert, New York
Pvt. 318 Sup, Co, QMC
March 20, 1941

Surprisingly, Henry's stone has no date of birth. I wondered why? Who was he? How did he die? Was he an immigrant? He died several months before we entered World War II, on December 8, 1941. I continue to wonder.

In his book *The Uprooted*, Oscar Handlin stated, "Once I thought to write the history of the immigrants in American history. Then I discovered that the immigrants were American history."

Likewise, one can study immigration history in America just by looking at the surnames while walking through the different sections of the cemetery. In the old part, people are interred with English, German, African, and Irish names buried in the 1860s, 1870s. In the newer sections are people with Irish, Italian, Polish, and Russian surnames from the 1880s to the present.

Judging from surnames in the newest section of the cemetery, the whole world is buried here: Koreans, Chinese, Spanish, and Latinos, people from all over the world. Each tombstone is a document of immigration history. The memorials tell our story, the story of the American people. The United States is the history of immigration. The immigrants are American history. Then, there are monuments, statues, headstones, mausoleums, and flat grave markers. There is a life-size statue of a Doughboy killed in World War I:

Joseph Anthony Jacobs

Pvt. 19 Co. Med, 52 Dept B Ric

Born Oct 1, 1895 – Died Dec. 17, 1918

This monument is a touching reminder of a horrible war. The irony is that it was referred to as "The War to End All Wars," or "The War to Make the World Safe for Democracy." This is a stunning representation of a WWI soldier who died 100 years ago. Walk through any cemetery, anywhere, and you will discover soldiers who gave their last full measure of devotion for America.

There are many graves of soldiers who died in different wars: the American Civil War, the Spanish–American War, WWI, WWII, the Korean War, Vietnam, Afghanistan, Iraq, and present-day conflicts.

Civil War 1861 – 1865

Mother Mary De Chantal Keating

Served as a nurse and hospital director, Wheeling, West Virginia, caring for both Union and Confederate soldiers. Awarded a medal for meritorious service by the Grand Army of the Republic 1904 (interred in Division Number 6)
*Saint Mary's Cemetery pamphlet 08/2013

Every time I enter the cemetery, passing Father Zanon's resting place in Mary Gate of Heaven Mausoleum conjures up feelings of reverence for a man who indeed served God and country:

WWII 1941 – 1945 and Korean War 1950 – 1953
Father Romano A. Zanon, Chaplain

Served in both Wars, awarded citation for meritorious services with the 8th Army in Korea, and also earned the Korean Service Ribbon with Silver Star. (entombed in Mary Gate of Heaven Mausoleum)
*Father Zanon served God, and country with faithful zeal (The Tablet 10/10/2018)

One grave in particular that stays with me is:

U.S.M.C.L/CPL Charles William Eglin, III
Killed in action, Vietnam
06/02/1947 – 02/15/1968

I went to school with Charles Eglin, III, PS 14 and Junior High School 16 in Corona, Queens. We called him "Chucky." I knew Chucky most of his short life. We played street games in Corona, and we hung out in Corona Heights. There was a pool hall on the corner of 52nd Avenue, where Corona Avenue merges with 108th Street. The pool hall was in the basement of Leppel's Department Store. I remember one time that I tried to pull a joke on Chucky. I brought an old *New York Times* newspaper with the heading, "Japanese Sneak Attack on Pearl Harbor!" Chucky got so upset, thinking this was a new and real crisis. Of course, I told him that it was only an old newspaper. But, now, many years later and more mature, I see that I shouldn't have made such a cruel joke.

Chucky loved our country dearly and made the ultimate sacrifice for it.

He was kind-hearted, but most of all, he was my good friend. I still miss him. He had a pleasant and pleasing personality. He was a wholesome fellow with a big smile, and everyone who met him liked him. He was well respected. He was the type of person who would help anyone and everyone. He was reliable, trustworthy, and kind. Chucky had a Mississippi accent, having been born and raised in Mississippi until he was an adolescent. I can still hear his voice. It rings with mellow Mississippi joy.

One wonders what Chucky's life would have been like had he survived. Would he have had children? I cannot fathom the loss of such an innocent twenty-one-year-old man from Corona. What does a Corona boy know about fighting in a jungle and the rice paddies of Vietnam? The people of Corona probably never heard of Vietnam before the war, and tens of thousands of our boys were shipped off approximately eight thousand six hundred and forty-four miles away, without much support from their government and the liberal news media.

My two brothers enlisted in that war. I tried to, but I was declared 4F because of a childhood illness, so I was spared the ordeal that so many of my friends and neighbors had to endure. Some were killed in action, never to return. I know ten soldiers from my neighborhood of Corona who were killed in action. Many of the returning soldiers were treated terribly! The media and a not-so-kind public handled our troops like the enemy. I paid homage to them here in Mount Saint Mary and Corona where they are memorialized in Ten Heroes Plaza, a triangle-shaped park at 108th Street between Van Doren Street and Westside Avenue. Only Charles William Eglin III is buried in the cemetery where I go walking.

I regret that so many boys had to die over there. Now, I try to honor those who served. I am happy to be alive. I went on to college, and became a teacher, poet, and historian who has traveled all around the world. I am happily married, healthy, and enjoying life. I am sorry for Chucky and so many others who did not make it home and have the same opportunity to live a full life as I have. It has been fifty years since Chuck's death. I still feel as if it was only yesterday.

On Memorial Day, I placed this poem on his grave:

Memorial Day Is Every Day

Memorial Day is every day when you have lost
a son,
daughter,
father,
mother,
husband,
wife,
brother,
lover,
friend.
Someone who made your day
who filled you with joy is now nothing but a void no one
    can ever fill,
like a hole in a passing cloud, it is now empty, not whole.
And then,
there are the anniversaries, holidays
and particular songs that awaken a heart in touching the
    throbbing pain.
You are but a shadow I cannot hold.
But oh!
Someone you can never share memories with ever again.
The image seared into my brain, my very soul.

Thinking of my friend Charles William Eglin, III, may you
"Rest in Soft Peace!" Chucky, I will stop at your grave
again the next time I go walking.

*

I have friends all over the United States who have families buried here. One dear old friend, Ms. Christine Trotta Bell, depends on me to act as caretaker of her parents' grave:

Loving Mother	Loving Father
Alba Bertocci	Salvatore Bertocci
1921 – 2009	1915 – 1991

The Bertocci family were my neighbors when I resided at 108-16 48th Avenue in Corona, Queens. They lived next door on a hill. Their lovely daughter, Christine, became my lifelong friend. I make sure the grave is kept manicured, handsome, and every holiday, I dress it up for the occasion. I emailed Christine all of my photographs. Remembering her parents makes her content and happy.

Another dear old friend of mine is Magdalen Bednarski. She is called Maggy. We both resided in the Murray Hill section of Flushing, Queens, on 150th Street, where her mother, Eugenia, was my mother's good friend. I knew Maggy's father, Frank, also. Maggy's parents were helpful and kind to me in my youth. Maggy and I have been good friends for over fifty years. Maggy is not always able to visit her parents' grave. So, I sometimes stop to pay my respects and place a stone on their grave. I do this to let everyone know that they will never be forgotten. Someone has visited their grave, making Maggy happy too. Their gravestone reads:

BEDNARSKI

Eugenia   Frank

1914 – 1977   In God's Care   1908 – 2000

One of my dearest and longtime friends, Ms. Carol Bozzo-Mozzone's mother, Frances Franz-Bozzo, has not yet been acknowledged. Frances Franz-Bozzo was a mother of five children: Joseph, Marianne, Carol, Michael, and Jacqueline. Frances was a loving mother, a community activist on the school board's Parent–Teacher Association, and a caring, loving human being who opened her home to me as a young boy. Her whole family became my friends. Frances's tombstone simply reads:

FRANZ

Beneath every stone is a story that speaks to us. If we forget the dead, the dead die a second time, forever forgotten. The deceased will always live as long as we tell their stories. Pondering on the demise of others makes one aware of our own mortality, creating feelings of compassion, empathy, fear, sympathy, understanding, and appreciation for life. Honoring the parents of friends who cannot make the journey is cathartic for our friends because they know someone has remembered their loved ones.

HISTORY IS ALIVE IN A CEMETERY

A cemetery is a work in progress, a manuscript of life unfolding before our very eyes. Still, one can acquire much knowledge about the past in a cemetery. Every tombstone tells a story, reflects a unique period in our history, and is a cultural icon and status symbol in our society. A cemetery is a timeline of the past, the present, the future. The interred represent history. A cemetery is a place where one can encounter people who may soon bud and bloom into friends. It is a place for the living to have a resting place with dignity, elegance, and grace when they depart. This Garden of Eden will continue the narrative of the soon-to-be-deceased, someday. However, for now, the cemetery is a living museum, and a discovery center.

Walk with me into this garden and see what I see. Only human beings can connect a concept to an object. The object becomes a symbol and takes on a unique meaning and history that's all its own. Many objects are symbols. Look at all the American flags, potent symbols, that conjure up strong feelings. Three symbols seared into my mind, heart, and soul are the Purple Heart placed on LCPL U.S. Marine Michael D. Glover's tombstone, a motorcycle helmet that rests on top of a headstone, and a toy military tank followed by lead soldiers in battle formation on another gravestone.

The Purple Heart on U.S. Marine Michael D. Glover's gravestone led me to these questions: Why was it placed there? Who set it there? Was it a sign of deep respect? Was it a sign of anger, contempt, or disdain? And then there is the question of who stole his Purple Heart, and why? Can it be replaced? Will it be replaced? These were the questions that came to mind when I saw that Purple Heart.

Touched by my discovery of the Purple Heart on U.S. Marine LCPL Michael D. Glover's tombstone and my encounter with Mrs. Glover, his mother, standing at her son's gravesite, I decided that I would work for world peace and spare another mother's son such a fate.

Another object that got my attention a decade later was the motorcycle helmet, found resting on a tombstone. It caught my attention because I thought it was a World War I helmet. What did I know before talking to anyone connected with the motorcycle helmet? Every time I passed the grave and saw something in the sunlight that beamed off rays of light, creating a *heiligenschein* sheen, but I did not stop to investigate.

Several weeks later, I noticed a man with his motorcycle standing at the same gravesite. I just kept walking, but I wondered about the object on the tombstone. What is it? Who placed it there? Why? How long has it been on this tombstone? I thought, "What if someone steals it?"

A week later, I heard music coming from a Humvee. The door was open. A man was sitting with his legs spread wide open, protruding outside the Humvee door. I wondered what he was doing. I cautiously walked up to him, recognized the object as a helmet, excused myself, and asked whether he knew anything about the helmet.

He told me, "Yes, it was my cousin's. He was killed in a motorcycle accident. He was only twenty-nine years old."

I expressed my sympathy. I told him I thought the helmet was from World War I, and he laughed and said, "No. Mr. Diaz was not only my cousin but he was also my best friend, and that was his helmet. We were all part of a motorcycle group."

I asked, "Aren't you afraid someone might steal the helmet?"

He said, "Hope not. I don't think so. It's been here for over a year."

Funny. Never noticed the helmet on my walks before until I was researching World War I, and then the helmet just appeared out of nowhere. Weeks later, the helmet was still resting on the same tombstone.

I continued on my walk and now came to Object Number 3. On top of this gravestone were lead soldiers in battle formation behind a toy military tank. I wondered what it was for. Was someone lost in war, or just a child at play? Did the tank and soldiers have meaning in the real world? I don't know why I never walked up to the gravesite to find out. Perhaps, one day, I will step up to the grave.

Three weeks later, I saw a little boy running to his father's grave. "Daddy! Daddy! Look what I have for you!" And he placed several lead soldiers in the back of a toy military tank. I was deeply touched. It is interesting that a little boy would give up his toys for his father. The little boy was probably around six years old. Guess that's why I could not walk to the grave to find out. I want to think that the little boy was just a child at play and nothing more.

A cemetery is a collection of information. True stories and real people. I keep thinking of the young boy with the toy military tank, which reminds me of another incident some twenty years ago, about another little boy sitting at his father's grave just after his father's burial. I penned the following poem, which captures that event:

A Little Boy Sitting on a Grave

A little boy sitting on his father's grave in the heat of the
  Sun
Sinking in the green grass silent as a flower
His knees folded elbows bent as if in sleep
Frightened fearful frozen
Soon he will get up to run and play.

Now I think I will walk over to the other side of the cemetery and take in some cemetery art.

Mausoleum Stained-Glass Window

THE CEMETERY IS AN ART GALLERY

The cemetery is an art gallery. Many monuments are extraordinary. Several stained-glass windows in mausoleums are fantastic and tell biblical stories; others reflect rustic, natural settings; still, others are glass gardens. A few stained-glass windows capture more than the light and will-of-the-wisp. They set the mood for peace, serenity, love, and beauty.

Passing a mausoleum on a cold winter's day, thirty years ago, I was stunned by the beauty of a stained-glass window. I stopped and penned a poem:

Spring Narrative in Glass

Walking through a cemetery,
Saw life is a stained-glass window.
It is seamed together like cell membranes.
Shards of glass are a heart beating forcefully.

Sunlight is its blood,
giving life, in rainbow-colored light.

Pulsating colors scream.
Rushing blue-green waterfalls splash through hills,
    valleys.
Hummingbirds hover over flowers.
Variegated pink trees blush.

Everything comes alive on a cold winter's day,
or a rich golden moonlight, shining in the dark of night.

A mausoleum window is such a sight few will see.

Another day in a Catholic tomb.

Amazing even the tombs speak to us, the living, about those entombed there. The massive mausoleums and memorial tombs reflect the baroque, art-nouveau, and art-deco periods. The stained-glass windows conjure up the work of Louis Comfort Tiffany and his fantasy colored glass...

Tiffany's Colored Fantasy Glass of Corona

Bubbles, blown firing hot,
glass fused, memories molded, shaped,
rays of light step out of lotus flowers,
hallucinating floating freely.

Mysteries magic mix, bronze-glass forever fixed,
blending rainbow's splendor.
Peacock-green, gold, silver-blue, red, star-white,
green, greenest green.
Swirling sunset, orange light,
jeweled ribbon ruby red, Favrile-white.
Colors frolic charming view,
Iridescent, vibrant bright.

Look, a fantastic marble statue of a kneeling woman is on a grave. Her hands hug the tombstone; her head rests on top of the headstone; her hair drapes over the monument; a rose is cupped in her praying hands. This heart-wrenching, art-deco statue, circa 1920, stands out from most of the monuments because it is so human, real, theatrical, and timeless. It reflects strong feelings of love, grief, and something more that one cannot put into words. There are other memorials with large bronze sculpted doors. They speak to us. They are sturdy and majestic, with depictions that make a statement. Look who resides here! Such displays of wealth and prestige try to reclaim one's station, status, and stature in society.

Every tombstone speaks to us. Walking along in the cemetery, I notice various bright flowers mirrored in black marble, and deep red rose bushes, contrasted against shrimp-colored headstones. All add to the orchestra of colors, like an art gallery. Even the grass is sometimes greener than green. Call it an Irish Garden. The sounds of singing birds and sweet scents fill the air like a petrichor smell after the rain. The sun twinkles between branches, tombstones, and mausoleums, playing hide-and-seek. The trees are of many species. Their leaves sway like hair in the breeze of many colors. Even fresh dirt smells clean. Life is everywhere. This art garden makes me want to be buried here under a tree.

Bury Me Under A Tree-II

My tombstone reads, Hello-Take a Seat-Stay a While
I bought a burial plot with a tree on it
Here I will spend eternity
Magnificent spread majestic sight crowned in stippled
    light

Fall much delight in pageant foliage splendid
    masquerade
Sea of leaves gently blanket
Where I lay protect me from ice in cold Winters

Winter trees exposed to knots and snarls
Bare, gnarled elbows wrinkled knees disrobed smiling
A graceful wild tree looks over me
Confronts the wind but does not give in-

In a massive snowstorm, she bears much weight
Knowing when to bend and not to break
Morning of Winter's moisture crystallized white
Moonlit trees dance dashingly between shadows

Spring seeds sprout and tips of stems bloom fruit and
    flowers
Songbirds sing perched on branches
Roots of trees reach out above branches shelter me
Summer canopied by leaves with veins of life sweet dew
oozing out scented sugar sap
God's sweet syrup life transplanted in a natural habitat
Is where I want to be when it is my time to depart

Bury me under a tree.

Remarkable that seeing trees change with the seasons is part of the cycle of life. Trees divested of their foliage, exposed knots, and snarls are as impressive as a tree in full summer's dress. Spring's orchestra of colors—the gorgeous, stunning sight makes one have a reverence for nature. Buried under a tree is where I want to be when I depart. To experience the bucolic beauty in nature to the fun of icons that grace a grave: all are part of the cemetery experience and add humor, charm, joy, speaking to us, making connections between the living and the dead.

I noticed many folk-art displays, reminders of the dearly departed. I call this memorial art, folk art, art for the living, in memoriam to the dead, or cemetery art.

There are colorful balloons, stuffed animals, frogs, turtles, owls, and birds. All add to the fantasy of life.

As I continued walking, I noticed one tombstone that broke my heart. It was made of black marble and engraved in vibrant and gleaming gold. It reads:

Patrick Kearney
May 10, 1895 – May 12, 1895

Patrick was just two days old, yet he has a name. For the first time on my walks through the cemetery, I felt deeply saddened. It brought back personal memories. The loss of a child for any parent, for anyone, is just too much to bear. I jogged around the cemetery twice, never to return to that gravesite again. When I go walking, I avoid this part of the cemetery. It's simply too hurtful.

ENCOUNTERS IN THE GARDEN OF EDEN

I have had many encounters in the Garden of Eden, various meetings with people of different races, ethnicities, classes, occupations, and backgrounds. Over the past three decades, as I walk or jog through the cemetery's meandering pathways, I have had some pleasant surprises and some encounters that have helped create lifelong friendships; others, hopefully, will ripen into friendships, in the coming years. However, some people will never open up because they choose to isolate themselves.

One man, in particular, seems estranged from the world. He will nod his head and say "Hello" and nothing more. This unknown man appears to be a specter. He sits at the same gravesite every afternoon between the hours of two and five until the cemetery closes. Sitting in a folding chair at the same grave, every afternoon, every day of the week; I assume it is his plot. He is either reading a book, praying, or gardening. He does not let people enter his world. So, I speedily pass him.

Walking up a hill in the direction of the crucifix, I noticed a large group I supposed was a family. Six ladies laid several colorful blankets on a grave. Out of straw baskets came the food: containers of rice and beans, meat and vegetables, fruits, water, iced tea, and soda, too. As the children ran around playing, the ladies sat on the blankets and distributed paper dishes, knives, forks, and spoons. Some ladies and men were walking around the grave plot. Others stepped up to the headstone, bowed their heads, and prayed. Children ran freely, laughing, and playing games. It was a picnic at a gravesite. The whole group seemed to be enjoying themselves, not mourning or grieving.

They were celebrating the life of the deceased and the life of the living, as they honored the dead. I could not contain my curiosity. So, delicately I worked my way toward the group, and said, "Hello. Are you having a picnic?" They replied, "This is a Filipino tradition. We were celebrating an anniversary. Told before by a director of the cemetery that such activities at a gravesite were not permitted or allowed. So, we are here on a Sunday when the office is closed, and we can practice an ancient tradition the way we did in the old country." They asked if I would like to join them in eating. I said thank you, but declined.

I was amazed to see such love, joy, and sorrow occurred at the same time. It was sad. It was sweet. Witnessing how this unique group of people paid reverence to the dead and enjoyed life at the same time. It is always interesting to me to see how differently people grieve and deal with their loss. This Filipino tradition is really for the living to help them cope with their loss in a family setting, with friends, as a social network.

As I walked away, I thought that this was a spiritual tradition. Why wouldn't these people be allowed to perform such a ritual at the gravesite of their dearly departed? I wondered if they would eat all the food on the blankets. Witnessing a ritual event was my cemetery adventure for the day; I kept on with my daily walk, expressed my sorrow for their loss, and I waved goodbye as I moved on.

Then, there are four people whom I would like to get to know. There are three women and one man whom I see from time to time walking or jogging the cemetery path. I don't always see them, as they walk on different days and not every day, and at different times. I am trying to work it out so I might see them on the trail. The few times I have encountered them, they were always very receptive, talkative, and friendly.

I hope to meet them again soon. The joggers' names are Rose, Mary, Laura, and William C. I don't know much more about them other than it is always a pleasant experience running into them. I hope to learn more about them and get to know them. It is still excellent to meet people and make new friends. I should have given them my business card with my email address and phone number. Maybe next time!

I resumed my walk and passed my Aunt Flo's grave. She is buried here, too. Aunt Flo took her life, so I penned this poem for her:

Aunt Flo's Goodbye

Aunt Flo had a daughter,
she was a drug addict.
Aunt Flo had leukemia,
her husband left her.

Aunt Flo had a party,
invited everyone she knew,
gave everyone gifts,
told everyone how much she loved them.

Aunt Flo said she was going on a trip.
She was found hanged!

Aunt Flo, I wish I could have helped you. I miss you. I cannot understand why anyone would not want to live and instead, take their life. Aunt Flo, I hope you are in peace in this lovely garden. I never knew you were in such psychological pain struggling not to give in to suicide. Life is so worth living. I want to enjoy all that life has to offer.

The cemetery serves as a footnote to life. Every day, walking through the cemetery, I have acquired compassion, empathy, sympathy, love, peace, and something new about all the people I've encountered.

At the cemetery just the other day, I met a colleague from Francis Lewis High School named Mr. Mason. I knew almost nothing about him, except that he is a great art teacher. Whenever I saw him in the hallways at Francis Lewis High School, he was always friendly. I once met him, his lovely wife, and his two charming children at an outing at the Hall of Science in Corona. Today, we, the Mason family and I, walked to his mother's grave:

Agatha T. Mason
06/03/1935 – 05/15/2006

I bowed my head and said a prayer, hoping she will rest in soft peace. Then he told me about his aunt:

P.O. Milagros Teresa
11/15/1966 – 11/11/1992
Badge# 4944

She was the first and only African American New York City Police Officer to protect Pope John XXIII when he performed a mass in Yankee Stadium, to an audience of tens of thousands of people. She was killed in the line of duty on November 11, 1992, years after she was assigned to protect the Pope.

I expressed my sympathy, appreciation, and amazement concerning Mason's aunt. Standing at her gravesite, his two girls were playing games, unaware of the somber circumstances. They were rolling down the hill, a grassy knoll. Such a delightful sight to see children at play. It is always a joyful thing.

Then they ran up to us and asked me how old I was. I said I was seventy.

They replied, "Is that why you are so short?"

I laughed, and Mr. and Mrs. Mason apologized profusely. "No need to apologize. They are just children," I said. Out of the mouths of children spout unfiltered thoughts. I brushed it off, laughing.

*

Today is a lovely day in June. The birds are singing. It is delightful, peaceful, and enjoyable to visit the garden on such a perfect day. Think I will sit under a tree. Thought about my final exit and how I should prepare for my wake and funeral, and why.

So, I began to think about that event, but first, I needed to speak to Sylvia, my wife. In the interim, I wrote a poem:

At My Funeral

Don't cry or lament; this is a poetry event.
Remember, while I lived, I loved poetry.
So, everyone who attends my funeral will read a poem!

Let me not lie in repose.
Make me want to get up from my deathbed.
Let the funeral parlor swing in a slam or Gothic poetry.
Show the world I once lived.
Hear my poetry.

I never died!
Read my poems and burn vanilla incense.
Please don't sing "Amazing Grace."
Play Whitney Houston's "Star-Spangled Banner."

On my grave, read Langston Hughes' poem, "Not What
   Was."
After the funeral, serve strawberries with whipped
   cream and champagne.

Heard a buzz saw echo. Was it a worker pruning trees? The smell of burnt wood and cut grass wafted through the air. Sounds grinding, grating, and creaking as spinning blades are whirling. An engraving, chisel power tool cuts deep, an inscription on a headstone takes on a new life. Hissing steam cleans tablets of marble, washing years of dirt and grime away. Gray becomes white, and stains disappear. They call this perpetual care. Flags flap in the wind over the city of the dearly departed. The sound of rustling leaves and the crisp crackling of bark stepped on, crushed, as people meander by. The subtle tone of footprints. Listen.

Hearing running water from a water tap is the sound of life. Water is life. The water flows, trickles, and splashes, forming a puddle where birds can play. From the trees, dropping acorns stopped with a thud when they hit the ground, sounds like raindrops, and the wind blows softly. These are the quiet sounds of a cemetery, and they do not seem to wake the dead. The sounds from the graveyard speak of the charm of the day.

Now, I will have to talk to Sylvia about our trip of a lifetime: our departure.

OUR LAST CURTAIN CALL

Walking through the cemetery today, I thought again about my departure, our last curtain call, but first, I had to convince Sylvia that it was something we should talk about, and how we should prepare for our wakes and our funerals. We decided my burial would be a poetry event. Sylvia's would be a simple, dignified service. Because we are of different faiths and races, we felt a non-sectarian cemetery would be more inclusive and accepting.

We spoke about prearranging our funerals. Sylvia wanted no part of it. I told her how important it was for us because I had the experience of burying four family members and was trying to spare her the anguish, grief, and pain of such an ordeal. We decided to make our wakes and funeral events and burials something we could both control while we are still alive, something memorable, humorous, and unforgettable. Had to convince Sylvia. Prearranging would be a benefit for both of us. We'd be planning now for our eternal future.

First, we had to purchase a plot. Sylvia loves gardening. So, we decided to buy a plot in a cemetery that was a garden. We selected a non-sectarian cemetery because we thought it would be preferable for us. Yes, a grave in a cemetery is a garden, with trees, rolling hills, and meadows. We wanted a plot on a hill under a tree with a dominant view and with an upstanding memorial. My love for trees caused me to write this poem:

Hello, I Am a Tree

You need me
It does matter what you think of me
I have my roots planted in mother earth
I'm gripping her by the waist with much love

Water is my life's blood
It seems the sun screams to hug my trunk
helping me sprout straight and grow in strength
I dress the lands in layers of loving long hair

I climb the mountains flirting with the light
I keep earth's soil in its place
and mark the ground in elegance and grace

Hello
I am a tree

We found a splendid place. We purchased just the right plot, Section 8, Division C, Plot 7, Grave 11. It is under a substantial towering golden-white oak tree high on a hilltop blanketed by wild garlic plants, bright with various variegated flowers. We fell in love with the spot! We now own a plot of land in a garden in New York City. We still had to purchase a memorial stone fit for such a bucolic pastoral setting.

We bought an ebony marble high-standing tombstone. The stone is in the shape of an open book. It is titled "The Book of Life." We had the stone engraved. The stone reads: "Hello. Take a Seat. Stay a While."

Every time the sun shines on our stone, it creates a mirrored image of the flowers and garlic that surround it. We are now both very pleased with our purchases. Yes, Sylvia always wanted a garden. She loves colored flowers, and we both love garlic. Often, we visit our plot. Sylvia works on gardening, and I sit under a tree reading poetry. Afterward, we walk the trails as part of our exercise routine.

Now, we had to decide on arranging our prepaid funerals. We visited a funeral parlor on Northern Boulevard in Flushing, Queens, to choose natural, attractive, and comfortable caskets. We picked cherrywood caskets. I have a reverence for wood; Sylvia loves cherries. I wanted to try the coffin out for size and comfort. The funeral director would have no part of this. I was persistent; Sylvia was embarrassed. I told the funeral director, "If I can't try it out, I will go somewhere else. I want to test it. After all, I will be spending the rest of my other life in it lying in repose." Finally, he yielded to my request but pleaded that we keep it a secret. Sylvia was aghast. I explained to her I wanted to be comfortable in my sleep of eternity.

Although the funeral director was reluctant, he said I could climb into the casket. I jumped into my future home and requested a fluffy fleece lining to fit my size, needs, and comfort. He accommodated me. Being inside the coffin was like being in a hammock: easy to climb in, hard to get out. I could hear my heartbeat. And then I almost fell asleep. Sylvia demanded I get out immediately. Then she asked if I was comfortable. Sylvia said she couldn't look at me in that position in a casket.

We finally purchased two caskets and arranged for our wakes and funeral events. Sylvia just wanted a quiet, elegant wake with a traditional funeral and burial with many-colored flowers. I told the funeral parlor director I wanted my wake to be a poetry reading event, where everybody who attends my funeral must read a poem. Vanilla incense and music will accompany the viewing. After the reading of poetry in the wake, everyone will be served champagne with strawberries and whipped cream.

At my Life After Death Ceremony, everyone will be given a black Mickey Mouse hat with big ears and different colored balloons. On my grave, Langston Hughes' poem, "Not What Was," will be read, as well as two poems that were written by me. After the burial, everyone will sing the Mickey Mouse Clubhouse theme song and let the colored balloons go. The funeral will proceed with a walk around the cemetery. Then, everyone will be sent home with my poem "9.11.01 (Poem Two)" on a memorial card so they have a keepsake to remember a patriot. This poem is placed in a pocket in the back of this book.

Afterward, everyone is invited to a banquet celebrating Death: "The Trip of a Lifetime."

*

Now that we have prepared for the future, we are back in the present, enjoying all the beauty around us. It's a beautiful day in July. The birds are exceptional today. A gaggle of birds sounded like an orchestra as they hopped and pranced from tombstone to tombstone. Some birds just perched high on top of headstones singing. How ironic for the cemetery to be so alive. The singing birds sound like organ music emanating from a cathedral. It fills the air with such joy.

It is beautiful to be active, alive, and taking in the fresh air, healthy, and happy. All that is missing in this garden cemetery is a pond and a water fountain. The sound of water sprouting up and cascading down is music to one's ears, magical and heavenly. Walking through the cemetery makes me realize how fortunate I am. Many of the interred here in this cemetery never had an opportunity to live a full life. One tombstone reads:

Sunset – Sunrise

1942   1942

One can only imagine what their lives would have been like if they had lived.

I passed my friend's grave, U.S.M.C.L/CPL. Charles William Elgin, III, and noticed an angel planter with cupped hands, an American flag, a gingerbread house, a butterfly on a rock labeled "Friends Forever," and a 1960's model Cadillac, and wondered who put them there and what they all symbolize.

Heard a thunderous screeching followed by a scraping noise. A tractor was dragging a huge boulder, which had been dug up from a grave. The rock was the size of my bathroom. It had crystal formations embedded in granite-like marble. A stunning stone. This boulder gleamed in the sun, creating a Cellini's halo. Crystals formed a rainbow dazzle like the inside of a geode. I thought this would be a significant memorial monument. As I left the cemetery, I turned my head, and the massive boulder looked like an angel sitting on the sun. This was a hallelujah moment. This angel image filled me with joy and a profound sense of peace and comfort. At home that night I wrote this poem:

Angels

Saw a fog turn into angel's wings

heard sweet songs full of love

Peace on earth

Goodwill

Saw a fog lift the sick into heaven's golden gate

Saw a fog end war

And

Thousands of wildflowers grew

where poppies grow

saw a fog float on water parting the sea

and all the world came together

like feathers of fog floating into eternity

Saw a fog

Woke up

Angels at my feet

THE END DEPENDS UPON THE BEGINNING

In this final chapter, I want to tell you that there is no end to a story about cemetery friends. The cemetery tells a continuing saga of an ongoing life process. It starts with birth and ends with a new beginning. It is only proper and fitting to end this book with a scene from the memorial service of Father Zanon, the man who taught this author how to express feelings in poetry, in writing. He showed that there are genuinely exemplary human beings who care about the forgotten, oppressed, sick, old, and the dearly departed.

I want to talk about the chapel service in his honor, where Father Zanon so often officiated Mass for the dead. Although there was a small number of people present, it was a rewarding, heartfelt tribute to an exemplary man.

After Deacon Sal Hili said Mass on October 22, 2018, I was invited to the altar to read my homage to Father Zanon in a preface and a poem:

PREFACE

It was raining, and I was alone on my way to my mother's grave over thirty years ago. She had just been buried two days ago when I stopped in my tracks. I saw a priest standing behind a casket on a grave in the rain, all alone. A priest, a coffin, and no one else. I stopped to show my respect. I remained there for the whole service, standing in the rain. Afterward, Father Zanon asked me if I was family. I said, "No. I was on my way to my mother's grave." Father Zanon replied, "I would like to walk with you to your mother's grave and bless her." Who else would walk with me in the rain without an umbrella to a grave of someone he did not know. He blessed Mama in the rain, and this was the beginning of a long friendship.

Father Zanon
October 12, 2018

I met you over thirty years ago, giving last rites on a grave,
    in the rain, standing all alone behind a casket, in the
    rain.

I walked over to join in prayer to show respect.
No one should be buried all alone.
Where are all the people?
In life, not being remembered is such a shame.
Father, your sermon on that grave
was as if there were a thousand people present.
The deceased would be proud.
In the rain, your voice rose into the clouds.

I knew the raindrops were from God
to let us know no one is forgotten.
He shed His tears for those who are alone, never to be
    forgotten!

I will always remember that day, in the rain.
From that day on, I saw the sunlight.

Thank you, Father Zanon.

Afterward, each person gave a touching, warm, and sometimes humorous tribute before we proceeded to the mausoleum. Estelle Flores spoke truth-to-reason as she told of her relationship with Father Zanon during a time of horrific grief. Her homage celebrated compassion, love, and humanity. Then, there was Peter Cirolia, an old friend of the priest. He told a very human story of how they bonded. One could hear and feel the love in his voice.

Nathalie Fouyer, a Professor of Comparative Literature at Queens College, spoke in warm terms about her "Uncle Ray." How he prompted her on, to do well in her university studies. Ms. Nathalie Fouyer spoke of the friendly relationship she had with her uncle, Father Zanon.

Each person—the two Nathalies, Sandra, Estelle Flores, Mr. Dongho Lee, Deacon Jack Reichert, Peter Cirolia, Marie Mazzenga, Zora Sormeley—and I paid homage to Father Zanon in our own human and unique way. His ashes were entombed in the Mary Gate of Heaven Mausoleum, and in a glass cremation niche in full view, along with my preface/poem, his photo, a religious patch, and a rosary.

I lament one of the many people I met along the way, the Reverend Romano A. Zanon. I pay tribute to him here. He departed this world on October 5, 2018, but not before he helped, reached, and touched so many people.

*

One month after Father Zanon's death, the leaves were turning into an orchestra of splendid colors: red, orange, brown, rust, and gold. The man who never talked to me and has tried to avoid me passed me, waved vigorously in acknowledgment, turned, and smiled as I continued walking the garden pathways.

A Latino family was eating cake and sitting on foliage, beautiful deciduous sheets of blanketed falling autumn leaves that created a bed alongside a tombstone. I noticed the different tombstones and their different styles.

And then, there are the unmarked tombstones, in which names are not etched, or inscribed into metal, marble, or stone, in time, making them unknown, lost to memory, and history.

Death, to Christians, is a new beginning of life, and so, the story never ends.

ACKNOWLEDGMENTS

"Pieta" — *Poesia*, Indian Bay Press, Vol. V/ No.2, Spring, 2007

"Crucified" — *Illuminations* Literary Journal, July 2008

"Reflections on A Purple Heart" —
   The Rockhurst Review, 21ˢᵗ Edition, Spring 2008, Rockhurst University

Grandmother Earth XIX, 2012

America's Poetic Soul: The Anthology of Enlightened Poets of America, April 2016

The Stevenson's Collectable Museum

"I Visited the Grave of Marine Michael D. Glover" —
   Grandmother Earth XX, 2014

   America's Poetic Soul: The Anthology of Enlightened Poets of America, April 2016

Best Overall Free Verse: 25ᵗʰ World Congress of Poets

United Poets Laureate International: World Brotherhood and Peace through Poetry, July 24th – 28th, 2018, Bangkok, Thailand

"Memorial Day is Every Day" — Maspeth Memorial Day Parade (75th Anniversary of the USO), Sunday, May 28, 2017

"A Little Boy Sitting on a Grave" — *Poetic Matrix: A Periodic Letter.* On the Poetic Experience 1 of 4, September 1, 2001

"Tiffany's Colored Fantasy Glass of Corona" — Atlantic Pacific Press, Winter, 2009, vol. 2/No. 4

"Bury Me Under A Tree-II" — *The Storyteller,* July/Aug/Sept 2008

"Aunt Flo's Goodbye" — *Trajectory Journal* Editor's Choice Online, January 9, 2016

"9.11.01 (Poem Two)" — *The Neo-Victorian/Cochlea,* Vol. VI/No. 1, Spring/Summer, 2002,

The Poets' Podium, Vol/ 11/No.1, Sept 2003

The Sampler, Vol. 35, Fall, 2003
The annual anthology of the Alabama State Poetry Society

Delco Times Delco Daily Top 10 9/11 Poems Anniversary

Maspeth Federal Savings Bank Booklet/Pamphlet,
September 2013 – September 2018

Queens by The Minute Webpage 09/14/2014

*America's Poetic Soul: Anthology of Enlightened Poets
of America*, April 2016

"Hello, I Am A Tree" — *Silver Wings*, No. 136, June – July
2010

"Angels" — *San Francisco Peace and Hope: A Literary
Journal*, 2015

"Father Zanon" — *The Tablet*, October 13 – 19, 2018

Preface and Poem Father Zanon housed in the
mausoleum cremation niche of the reverend father
Romano A. Zanon, Mary Gate of Heaven Mausoleum,
Mount Saint Mary Cemetery

Quotes: Published Elsewhere

"Inside My Cozy Coffin," by Vincent J. Tomeo
I Claudius Speaks: January 6, 2017, In Essay Issue
No.3 online

"Our Prearranged Funerals," by Vincent J. Tomeo
Evening Street Review, No. 17, Autumn 2017

James Baker, Former Sec. of State Eulogy for President
George W.H. Bush, 12/06/2018

**For so many reasons, I want to thank the following
friends for their input and so much more:**

Cynthia Seibel
Joyce Cochran Jasiukaitis
Francine Reibman
Karen Wilczewski

9.11.01 (Poem Two)

I want to wrap myself
In the American flag
I want to fly high
I want to blow in the wind
I want to ripple in the light
I want to sing
God Bless America
I want to coil up
cry for those who gave their lives
I want to be forever free
I want to announce to the world
I am a native New Yorker
I am an American

This poem was written three days after 9/11 on September 14, 2001. Cut out this poem on the dotted line and keep it in your pocket or your wallet, or give it to a friend, a stranger, a compatriot.

ABOUT ATMOSPHERE PRESS

Atmosphere Press is an independent, full-service publisher for excellent books in all genres and for all audiences. Learn more about what we do at atmospherepress.com.

We encourage you to check out some of Atmosphere's latest nonfiction releases, which are available at Amazon.com and via order from your local bookstore:

White Snake Diary, nonfiction by Jane P. Perry

Giving Up the Ghost, essays by Tina V. Cabrera

Family Legends, Family Lies, nonfiction by Wendy Hoke

What?! You Don't Want Children?: Understanding Rejection in the Childfree Lifestyle, nonfiction by Marcia Drut-Davis

Peaceful Meridian: Sailing into War, Protesting at Home, nonfiction by David Rogers Jr.

Southern. Gay. Teacher., nonfiction by Randy Fair

Evelio's Garden, nonfiction by Sandra Shaw Homer

Heat in the Vegas Night, nonfiction by Jerry Reedy

To the Next Step, nonfiction by Kyle Grappone

ABOUT THE AUTHOR

Vincent J. Tomeo is a poet, archivist, historian, and community activist.

For 36 years, he taught American history at a New York City public high school. He has formerly volunteered at the 9/11 Tribute Center Museum at Ground Zero.

Vincent is published in the *New York Times, Comstock Review, Mid-America Poetry Review, Edgz, Spires, Tiger's Eye, ByLine, Mudfish, The Blind Man's Rainbow, The Neo-Victorian/Cochlea, The Latin Staff Review, The Evening Street Review,* and *Grand- mother Earth (VII thru XI).*

To date, Mr. Tomeo has 886 poems/essays published and has participated in 124 public readings. He is the winner of 105 awards, including The Best Overall Free Verse by United Poets Laureate International World Brotherhood and Peace Through Poetry, World Congress of Poets, Bangkok, Thailand, July 2018, and an Honorable Mention in the Rainer Maria Rilke International Poetry Competition 1999.

In February 2020, two of Mr. Tomeo's poems, "Belleau Wood 2020," and "Remembering A Corona Marine, US Marine, Private William Frederick Moore," will be distributed and read in schools as part of the Aisne-Marne Cemetery Project, Rue des Chevaliers Colomb, 02400 Belleau, France.

Figure 3. Mausoleum bronze door in the family name of Sheedy erected in memory of John Kelly Mount Saint Mary Cemetery, 172-00 Booth Memorial Avenue, Flushing, NY 11365

CPSIA information can be obtained
at www.ICGtesting.com
Printed in the USA
LVHW070616100620
657590LV00006BC/687